TSUNAMI!

The 1946 Hilo Wave of Terror

by Scott Ingram

Consultant: Daniel H. Franck, Ph.D.

BEARPORT
PUBLISHING COMPANY, INC.

New York, New York

Credits

Cover (all photos), Pacific Tsunami Museum Archives.

Title page, Pacific Tsunami Museum Archives; 4-5, Fumiko Hata Collection / Pacific Tsunami Museum Archives; 6-7, Louis Pappas and Monica Ponomarev; 9, Courtesy of the National Oceanic and Atmospheric Administration Central Library Photo Collection; 10-11, Howard Pierce Collection/ Pacific Tsunami Museum Archives; 12-13, Craig Aurness / CORBIS; 14-15, Pacific Tsunami Museum; 16-17, Aleta V. Smith Collection / Pacific Tsunami Museum Archives; 18, Pacific Tsunami Museum Archives; 19, Beago Collection / Pacific Tsunami Museum Archives; 20, Pacific Tsunami Warning Center / National Oceanic and Atmospheric Administration; 21, AP Photo/VIctoria Times Colonist, Ian McKain; 22-23, © Photo by Paul J. Buklarewicz; 24, Phil Schermeister / CORBIS; 25, Charles O. Cecil; 26, Adriel Heisey; 27, courtesy of Marie Eble, Pacific Marine Environmental Laboratory / National Oceanic & Atmospheric Administration; 29, Steve Wilkings / CORBIS.

Design and production by Dawn Beard Creative, Triesta Hall of Blu-Design, and Octavo Design and Production, Inc.

This book is dedicated to the memory of the people who lost their lives in the tsunami of December 26, 2004.

Library of Congress Cataloging-in-Publication Data

Ingram, Scott.
  Tsunami! : the 1946 Hilo wave of terror / by Scott Ingram ; consultant, Daniel H. Franck.
      p. cm. — (X-treme disasters that changed America)
  Includes bibliographical references and index.
  ISBN 1-59716-010-5 (lib. bdg.)—ISBN 1-59716-033-4 (pbk.)
  1. Tsunamis—Hawaii—Hilo—Juvenile literature. I. Title. II. Series.

  GC221.5.I54 2005
  363.34'9—dc22

                          2004020745

For more information, write to Bearport Publishing Company, Inc., 101 Fifth Avenue, Suite 6R, New York, New York 10003. Printed in the United States of America.

1 2 3 4 5 6 7 8 9 10

Table of Contents

Lenworthy 5/05

Fish Without Water

"The water is disappearing!" a worker yelled, early in the morning on April 1, 1946.

Tuck Lee heard the worker and ran to the **docks**. He had lived in Hilo (HEE-low), Hawaii, most of his life. He had never seen anything like this. The water had left the **harbor**.

▲ A 1946 photo of the tsunami rushing ashore near Hilo

4

Fishing boats tipped on their sides. The fish couldn't swim. Some workers jumped off the wooden docks, grabbing the fish. Tuck Lee ran and climbed a ladder leading up to a tower. He knew something was very wrong. He was right. He saw a **tsunami** (tsoo-NAH-mee) headed for shore.

Hilo is on Hawaii. Hawaii is the largest of the eight main islands that form the state of Hawaii.

What Is a Tsunami?

A tsunami is one or more waves caused by an **earthquake** or a **volcano** erupting in the ocean. The Hilo tsunami began far from Hawaii, near the coast of Alaska. Deep under the ocean's **surface**, there was an earthquake. Water was pushed out from the center of the earthquake like ripples around a stone thrown in a pond.

Tsunami!

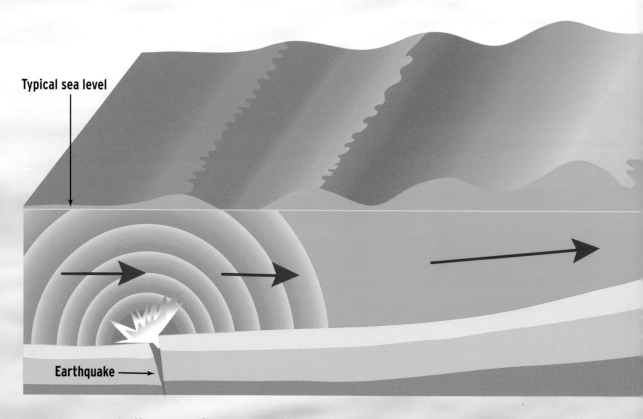

Typical sea level

Earthquake →

As the ocean floor rises, the waves quickly pile up. They build into a huge tsunami wave that crashes onto the shore.

The waves of a tsunami travel about 500 miles per hour. They're so deep they can move a thousand miles without being seen. When the waves reach **shallow** water, they pile on top of each other. The wall of water becomes a killer.

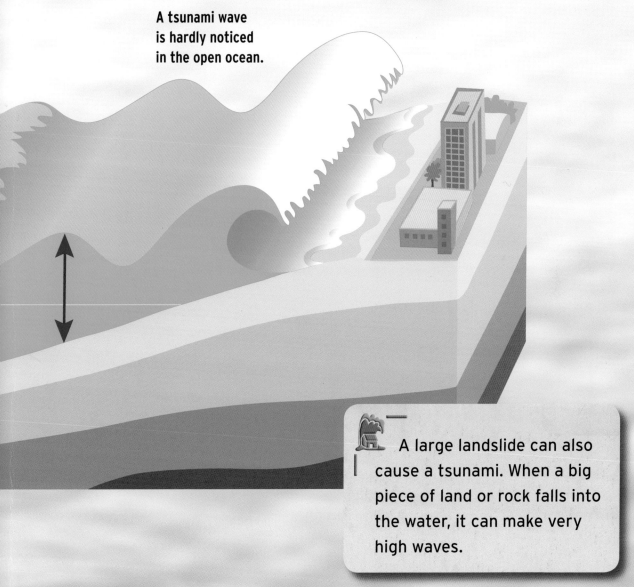

A tsunami wave is hardly noticed in the open ocean.

A large landslide can also cause a tsunami. When a big piece of land or rock falls into the water, it can make very high waves.

No One Left Alive

The tsunami on April 1, 1946, began just after midnight. The first people it killed lived in Alaska. They worked at a **lighthouse** called Scotch Cap. The lighthouse was 40 feet above the water and stood five **stories** high. An hour after the earthquake, a giant wave rose in the dark. It hit Scotch Cap hard.

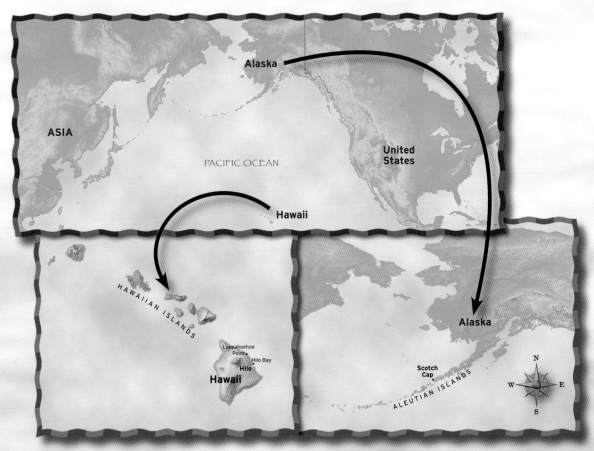

▲ An underwater earthquake near Alaska caused a tsunami that traveled across the ocean and hit Hawaii about five hours later.

All five people inside were washed away. The only people who knew about the tsunami were dead. No one was left to warn the people of Hilo as the waves traveled quietly and quickly across the ocean.

▲ Scotch Cap Lighthouse after the tsunami hit

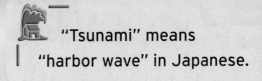

"Tsunami" means "harbor wave" in Japanese.

A Giant Mountain

Back in Hilo, a boy named Robert Fergustrom (FER-gus-trom) walked to school with his friends. The group stopped at a hill called Laupahoehoe (LOU-pa-HOI-HOI) Point. When Robert looked down at the harbor, he was puzzled. Where was the water? Then he looked up. The ocean had turned into a giant mountain. Robert had never seen anything so scary.

The water raced toward Hilo. Robert ran up the steps to the school. His friends ran slower. They hid in the stands near the baseball field. When Robert looked back he saw that the tsunami had swallowed the stands. His friends were gone.

A person should never go to a beach to watch a tsunami. Escape may be impossible.

▼ Laupahoehoe Point in 1946

Like No Other Wave

Most waves are caused by winds. On windy days, waves have white tops. It may take ten seconds for a wave to curl and **break** on the beach. Big storm waves can send water 300 feet across the sand. This distance is about as long as a football field.

▼ Normal waves hitting the shore in Hawaii

Tsunamis don't have white tops. When they reach shallow areas, they begin to take in calm water near the shore. They can keep pulling in water for an hour. By then, some tsunamis can be as tall as ten-story buildings. They may send water 1,000 feet across land when they break.

High tide is the time each day when water levels are highest on shore. Tides, however, have nothing to do with tsunamis. They're caused by the moon.

A Brown Wall

It was just after 7:00 a.m. at the Hilo docks, a mile from Laupahoehoe Point. Tuck Lee looked down from his seat on the high tower. Out beyond the harbor he saw a brown wall of water. He heard a sound like a screaming jet coming in for a landing.

The tsunami roared across the harbor. It snapped docks like twigs and threw boats on top of buildings. The pounding wave filled the streets and lifted up palm trees. Tuck Lee thought he was high enough to be safe. The water, however, was right below him.

◀ A man looks on as the tsunami hits Hilo in 1946.

A tsunami can also sound like a train whistle as it's about to hit.

Death at Laupahoehoe School

Robert Fergustrom was safe at Laupahoehoe School because it was far from the water. Some teachers and kids, however, were on their way to school. Robert's friend Masuo Kino (ma-su-o key-no) was one of those kids.

The water lifted Masuo up like a giant hand. It carried him headfirst toward a stone wall. He thought he was going to die. Somehow Masuo Kino lived. The wave hit the wall right in front of him. "I was rolling underwater with all the rocks," he said.

Many others weren't so lucky. The tsunami killed 16 students and five teachers.

◀ A tsunami wave strikes Coconut Island in Hilo in 1946.

Tsunamis can travel up rivers and streams that empty into the ocean.

Lucky Escapes

The wave hit homes and buildings in Hilo. James Low tried to drive to safety. Before he could start his car, the water reached his neck. He swam out of his car window.

▲ The Hilo tsunami arrives in 1946.

Back on the tower, Tuck Lee saw the water right below him. He was afraid. Then he saw a boat and decided to swim to it. It was like swimming through the sky. He was higher than any of the buildings.

Sailors threw him a rope and pulled him up. By the time a second wave hit Hilo's shore, Tuck Lee was safely on the boat.

The 1946 tsunami traveled 2,200 miles from Alaska to Hilo in about five hours.

◀ A student being lifted out of the water by a sailor after the tsunami hit. He was lost at sea for about 30 hours.

Tsunami Warning System

In 1948, two years after the Hilo tsunami, scientists set up the Pacific Tsunami Warning Center (PTWC) in Hawaii. The center uses special **instruments** called **seismographs** (SIZE-muh-*grafs*).

A seismograph's needle moves when an earthquake takes place. This motion shows the earthquake's power. With information from several seismographs, scientists can tell where the earthquake happened.

A tsunami is almost always caused by an earthquake. So, seismographs can warn scientists of tsunamis, too. When a strong underwater earthquake hits, scientists can figure out when and where a tsunami will happen. The PTWC uses **sirens** and radio **broadcasts** to warn people.

▲ This scientist reads a seismograph that shows an earthquake has just hit Victoria, Canada (2001).

The Tsunami Warning System was used when tsunamis struck Hawaii in 1952 and 1957. The system worked well.

Hilo Is Hit Again

On May 22, 1960, an underwater earthquake struck near South America. The warning center in Hawaii knew that a tsunami was racing toward Hilo. Sirens and news messages warned that the tsunami was 15 hours away. Hilo, however, had not been hit since 1946. People had forgotten the tsunami's power.

Many remained close to the ocean. They decided to take a chance. The tsunami hit when scientists thought it would. Just after midnight, it roared out of the dark ocean. Sixty-one people were killed. Large parts of Hilo were destroyed. The warning system worked, but people did not listen.

▼ Downtown Hilo in 1999

Tsunamis that cause damage strike Hawaii about every seven years.

Tsunamis: Keep Out!

After the tsunami in 1960, Hilo leaders took steps to make the city safer. They helped people who lost their homes rebuild on higher ground. They set aside new places for businesses that had been destroyed. Areas near the shore were filled with dirt. A wall 30 feet high was built at the shore.

▲ Stores were rebuilt after the tsunami.

Today, buildings stand behind the wall. Homes are built on high ground. Parts of Hilo that were once in danger are now part of a state park. People can ride their bikes there. At Laupahoehoe Point, a stone statue lists teachers and children killed in 1946.

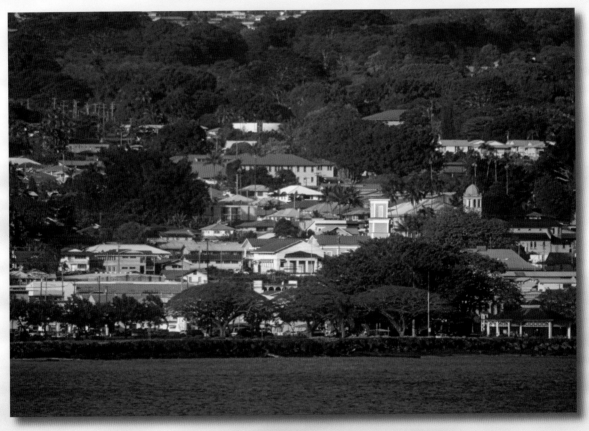

▲ Hilo, Hawaii, from across Hilo Bay

In Japan, concrete walls protect many cities. Huge gates also close to protect harbors.

Modern Tsunami Warnings

Groups of seismographs can tell when the earth moves. They don't always show, however, if a tsunami will happen.

▲ Instruments on the ocean floor sense tsunami waves.

Computers also use satellite information to tell when a tsunami will hit and how high it will be.

Today, instruments lie on the Pacific Ocean floor. They sense when a tsunami passes over them. They send a message to a **buoy** floating on the waves. The buoy sends the message to space **satellites**. From there, the information goes to warning centers. Computers then use it to find the path of the tsunami. These warnings are lifesavers.

RONALD H. BROWN

TSUNAMI

Just the Facts

The Hilo Tsunamis

- The tsunami that hit Hilo on April 1, 1946, came in two waves that were each 30 feet high.
- The 1946 tsunami killed 159 people and destroyed 1,300 homes.
- The tsunami that hit Hilo on May 23, 1960, was about 30 feet high.
- The 1960 tsunami killed 61 people and injured 282.

Tsunami Records

- The tsunami with the highest wave took place in Alaska on July 7, 1958. It was 100 feet tall.
- The deadliest tsunami on record struck South Asia on December 26, 2004. It was caused by a huge earthquake under the Indian Ocean. More than 100,000 people were killed.
- Japan is the country that has been struck most often by tsunamis. In the past 300 years, it's believed that there have been 250 tsunamis.
- Hawaii is the state hit most often by tsunamis.

Tsunamis Today

- There are now 26 Pacific Tsunami Warning System (PTWS) stations. These stations are along the Pacific Coast of the United States, Hawaii, and Japan.

- Today, the Hawaii warning center has a "tsunami watch" and a "tsunami warning." A "watch" lets people know that an earthquake has happened in the ocean. A "warning" lets people know that a tsunami might reach Hawaii.

- After a warning is made, sirens sound before the wave comes ashore. Three minutes later, special radio and television messages are broadcast. They let people know how large the tsunami will be and where it might hit.

- Many buildings in tsunami areas are now built with steel and concrete.

Glossary

break (BRAYK)   to crash into the shore

broadcasts (BRAWD-kasts)   television or radio programs

buoy (BOO-ee)   a floating object in the ocean that can send messages to space satellites

docks (doks)   landing areas where ships load and unload goods

earthquake (URTH-kwayk)   a sudden, violent shaking of the earth, caused by a shifting of the earth's crust

harbor (HAR-bur)   a protected part of a body of water where ships rest or unload goods

instruments (IN-struh-muhntz)   tools used by scientists and others for special work

lighthouse (LITE-houss)   a tower with a flashing light that guides ships at night or during heavy fog

satellites (SAT-uh-lites)   spaceships or other objects sent into space that send information back to earth

seismographs (SIZE-muh-*grafs*)   instruments that detect earthquakes and measure their power

shallow (SHAL-oh)   not deep

sirens (SYE-ruhnz)   pieces of equipment that make a loud, wailing sound

stories (STOR-eez)   floors of a building

surface (SUR-fiss)   the outside or outer layer of something

tsunami (tsoo-NAH-mee)   a huge wave or group of waves caused by an underwater earthquake or volcano

volcano (vol-KAY-noh)   a mountain that can erupt

Bibliography

Prager, Ellen. *Furious Earth: The Science and Nature of Earthquakes, Volcanoes, and Tsunamis.* New York, NY: McGraw-Hill (1999).

Robinson, Andrew. *Earth Shock.* New York, NY: W.W. Norton (1993).

Steele, Christy. *Tsunamis (Nature on the Rampage).* Austin, TX: Raintree (2001).

Van Rose, Susanna. *Volcano & Earthquake.* London, England: Dorling Kindersley (1992).

Read More

Sorenson, Margo. *Tsunami: Death Wave.* Logan, IA: Perfection Learning (1997).

Spilsbury, Louise, and Richard Spilsbury. *Sweeping Tsunamis (Awesome Forces of Nature).* Chicago, IL: Heinemann Publishing (2003).

Thompson, Luke. *Tsunamis.* New York, NY: Children's Press (2000).

Wade, Mary D. *Tsunami: Monster Waves.* Berkeley Heights, NJ: Enslow Publishers (2002).

Learn More Online

Visit these Web sites to learn more about tsunamis:

- http://observe.arc.nasa.gov/nasa/exhibits/tsunami/tsun_bay.html
- http://wcatwc.gov/tsunami1.htm
- http://www.fema.gov/kids/tsunami.htm
- http://www.tsunami.org/faq.htm

Index

About the Author

Scott Ingram has written more than 40 books for young adults. He lives in Portland, Connecticut, far from the danger of a tsunami.